THE
Archive Photographs
SERIES

SOUTHAMPTON

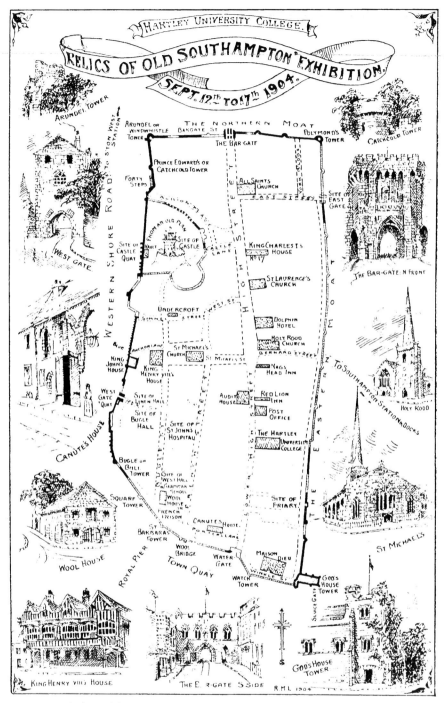

This neat pictorial plan of the medieval walled town by R.M. Lucas publicised the 'Grand Loan Exhibition of Relics of Old Southampton, illustrating the ancient life and history of the borough' staged at Hartley University College for a week in 1904. It is truly remarkable how many historic buildings have endured the ravages of time, war and redevelopment, surviving to link past and present.

THE
Archive Photographs
SERIES

SOUTHAMPTON

Compiled by
A.G.K. Leonard

CHALFORD

First published 1997
Copyright ©A.G.K. Leonard, 1997

The Chalford Publishing Company
St Mary's Mill, Chalford,
Stroud, Gloucestershire, GL6 8NX

ISBN 0 7524 0733

Typesetting and origination by
The Chalford Publishing Company
Printed in Great Britain by
Redwood Books, Trowbridge

Cover photograph:
Southampton girls on war work during the First World War (see p.116)

The success of the 1904 'Old Southampton' loan exhibition promoted a desire for the town to have its own permanent historical museum. This was eventually opened in 1912 in Tudor House, which the Council had been persuaded to acquire from Mr W.F.G. Spranger, for about half what he spent on it. Prior to his reconstruction around 1900, the town mansion built c. 1500 for Sir John Dawtry had declined in status and was subdivided into several separate commercial tenancies, as shown in this photograph, c. 1880. (Courtesy City Heritage Service)

4

Contents

Acknowledgements

Most of the illustrations in this book come from my own collection of postcards and photographs but some have been made available by kind friends and by departments of Southampton City Council. Grateful acknowledgement of their contributions is made to Jeff Pain, Jack Foley, Bob Payne, Derek Popplestone, John Stockley, Colin Townsend and to Tom Holder for photographic assistance. I am also indebted to Southampton Archives Service, Southampton Oral History Archive and the Local Studies Library at Southampton Central Library (including all their ever-helpful members of staff) for provision of research facilities, information and illustrations.

If we have inadvertently infringed anybody's rights in respect of photographic reproduction in these pages, compiler and publisher hope they will excuse us.

The twentieth-century appearance of Tudor House derives from Spranger's restoration work around 1900, an attempt to recreate the original Tudor façade. (The story is told in the booklet *The Saving of Tudor House* by the present writer)

6

Introduction

This selection of historic photographs illustrates aspects of the development and everyday life of Southampton from Victorian times to the outbreak of the Second World War.

During these years the town and port enjoyed almost continuous growth and prosperity, carrying forward the pattern of progress started in the 1750s. From being one of the country's leading medieval ports, Southampton had declined and stagnated in Tudor and Stuart times, until it later revived in a new-found role as a spa, sea-bathing and residential resort. This promoted a buoyant service economy, reflected in the doubling of its population in 1750-1800, to nearly 8,000 at the first census in 1801. Continuing growth took this figure to nearly 28,000 in 1841; the advent of railway and docks underpinned further increase, to over 60,000 in 1881. Incorporation in 1895 of the expanding suburbs of Shirley, Freemantle and Bitterne Park boosted the 1901 census figure to 105,000. The development of ship building and repairing, with light industries and other activities related to Southampton establishing itself as 'The Gateway to the World', brought further suburban growth and population increase. The 1920 boundary extension east of the Itchen, bringing in Bitterne, Itchen, Sholing and Woolston, carried the borough total to over 162,000 in 1921; it reached nearly 180,000 in 1931.

Before and between the two World Wars Southampton was clearly a flourishing and expanding place but contemporary photographs generally give an impression of tranquillity, which has enduring nostalgic appeal; they evoke a simpler and more leisurely pattern of life, most noticeable in the main streets, which often appear almost empty, although pedestrians are numerous. From 1900 municipally operated electric trams provided cheap and frequent public transport, while railways carried numerous short journey passengers as well as huge amounts of goods; motor vehicles only gradually displaced horse-drawn carts and vans or hand barrows for local deliveries and private cars were little used for getting to work or shops in the town centre.

One should not, of course, view the Edwardian and inter-war years as a sort of Golden Age. The lives of many people were frequently hard and insecure, with much sharper differences between rich and poor, in a more rigid class structure; apparent contentment was often dissolved by bitter industrial and political disputes.

A wealth of pictorial documentation, full of human interest, is provided by the work of contemporary photographers, primarily those who issued postcards, which in the nature of things have a higher survival rate. There were six photographers in Southampton in 1859; one was Joseph Latter, starting a family business at 13 Bernard Street which lasted until 1914, but this is largely forgotten because it published only a few printed shipping cards around 1910.

Professional photographers concentrated on studio portrait work; when cheaper ('pocket') cameras became available from the 1890s they were mainly used for family and holiday 'snaps'. Commercial possibilities for pictures of local streets, shipping, transport, topical events and occasions opened up around 1900, as postcards came into general use, providing cheap, simple and speedy means of everyday communication in an age of extending literacy and greater mobility for both work and leisure. National publishers produced millions of cheaply printed cards, often in poor quality colour; local enterprises contributed small editions of real photographic cards, now increasingly esteemed for their documentary value.

This book includes examples from more than a score of old-time Southampton photographers, selected with emphasis on less familiar topics and views. Numerous other Edwardian street scenes, transport and shipping subjects have been featured in the writer's earlier books; *Southampton in Old Picture Postcards*; *Maritime History of Southampton in Picture Postcards* and *Edwardian Southampton in Picture Postcards of F.G.O. Stuart*.

Doyen of local photographers and postcard publishers was the splendidly named Francis Godolphin Osborne Stuart (1842-1923), a Scot who settled in Southampton around 1883. As a 'landscape photographer' he ranged widely to supply illustrations to various local and national publications, building up a stock on which he drew to start issuing postcards in 1901. His output eventually exceeded 2,500. Stuart's best coloured cards of 1903-11, finely lithographed by the Leipzig firm of C.G. Röder, have greatest appeal to collectors but some of his monochrome and sepia real photograph cards contribute most significantly to the social history of his adopted town.

So also do the quality productions of another early card publisher, G. Whitfield Cosser, in business at Hanover Buildings *c.* 1902-5 and afterwards at Salisbury and Devizes. The market was big enough for him to sell prints of the same photograph several times over to various national publishers – usually for inferior coloured reproductions. Local contemporaries included Mentor & Co. with a studio in Oxford Street *c.* 1890-1908, and Mallett & Sons, briefly occupying one a few doors away around 1905. Much longer-lasting was the business of Max Mills, the trade name of Wilfred Ashby, talented artist and musician as well as photographer; he took over a studio in East Park Terrace in 1898, moving later to a new one in Rockstone Place, where he continued until 1939.

Adolphe Rapp traded in Bernard Street in 1908-14 as bookseller and marine photographer but he also produced souvenir and topical postcards, both to order and speculatively (pages 101-2). During the same period, John Oakley, based at Netley Abbey, did likewise, although specialising in photographs of troopships.

Miss G.A. Pratt, a 'nautical bookseller' in Oxford Street from 1910, issued shipping postcards but was not a photographer like Nellie G. Smith, who ran a high class studio in Commercial Road from 1912 into the 1930s: she produced postcards to private order. Among other town centre studios operating before and between the wars were those of George Applin, S.A Chandler & Co. and Short & Millard. Across the Itchen, James T. Eltringham, 'artist in photography' at Portsmouth Road, Woolston *c.* 1903-23, issued several hundred postcards of local scenes and events. Cycling around with his camera to record aspects of pre-1914 Southampton, Herbert Willsteed also left a valuable photographic legacy in postcards. These were a sideline to his job as a Royal Mail baggage handler; he had no studio, his cards being produced by a local chemist. Thomas Hibberd James, a bookseller in Bernard Street, used his camera to good effect around the town from the 1880s. W.M. Phillips of Hampton Park was not listed as a photographer but issued postcards as a sort of cottage industry, as did H.C. Brain of Shirley – where William Pearce had a High Street photographic business from 1908 but in the 1920s switched to running a fried fish shop!

Wholesale stationers in Bevois Valley Road, 1900-64, A.E. Rood/Rood Brothers distributed evocative views of Southampton before and after the First World War; the photographers remain unknown. Another pre-1914 postcard wholesaler was Clarence Bealing, who selectively ordered local scenes from various national publishers. Documentation of the great liners in their heyday was provided by some 300 glossy 'real photograph' cards published from 'No. 1 The Docks' through thirty years from 1924 by O.W. Hoffmann, first on behalf of his tobacconist father, then on his own account. Numbering enhances collector appeal and they are now much sought after, subject of detailed accounts in the 1989 *Picture Postcard Annual* and *Hampshire* magazine, July 1989.

One
Bygone Townscapes

A selection of street scenes in and around Southampton, from Victorian times to the years between theWars, evokes a vanished age when the pattern of town life was simpler and seemingly more leisurely. Main thoroughfares were busy enough with pedestrians and cyclists but appear curiously tranquil, with little traffic apart from horse-drawn cabs and carts and the trams (and buses from the 1920s) that provided the cheap and frequent public transport on which almost everyone relied to get to town for work or shopping. Even in the 1930s private motor cars were little used for such travel. Motor vans and lorries were slow to displace horse-drawn transport, while over longer distance goods were mostly carried by rail rather than road.

Any pictorial survey of Southampton must begin at the Bargate, the ancient fortified entrance to the medieval walled town that has endured through the centuries, still symbolising the modern city. Here is a unique representation of it, from a postcard photograph captioned 'Cork model by T.H.W. 1911.' Its fate and its maker's identity remain unknown.

Horse cabs, cycles and a tricycle around the south side of the Bargate, *c.* 1903. All traffic had to pass through its arch until new roads around it were created in the 1930s. G. Whitfield Cosser sold this photograph to several other postcard publishers. The building on the right accommodated the busy firm of J.J. Burnett & Sons, auctioneers, accountants etc. and forerunner of Burnett Swayne, who celebrated 150 years of business history in 1996.

Passing a man on his tricycle through the Bargate, two Edwardian ladies ride their bikes up Above Bar, keeping well away from the sunken tram tracks, a hazard for the wheels of unwary cyclists.

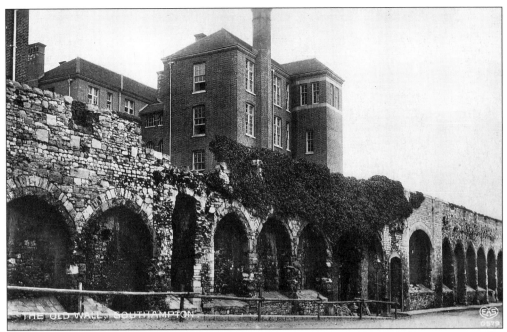

A selection of the wonderfully enduring old walls showing the fourteenth-century arcades strengthening the frontages of Norman merchants' houses incorporated into the town defences. Above them (often painted out for postcard pictures) are the incongruous red brick buildings of St Michael's House, a municipal lodging house, opened in 1899, demolished in 1972.

This view of the Western Shore, c. 1905, highlights the pre-reclamation waterfront, when Pickett's boatyard was still operational. The cannons, which went for scrap in the Second World War, were Crimean War trophies and old British 9-pounders, sometimes fired for special celebrations. The neat canopied drinking fountain is a 1901 memorial to Mrs Mary Ann Rogers, heroic stewardess of the steamer *Stella*, wrecked in the Channel Islands on Good Friday 1899.

An ice-cream barrow and a line of horse cabs at the bottom of the High Street, pre-1890, before the Castle Hotel (left foreground) was converted into offices; the Vine Hotel beyond it continued until bombed in 1940. Opposite, the Sun Hotel, another victim of enemy action, was quickly replaced by long-lasting 'temporary' wooded buildings, eventually demolished for site redevelopment in 1994.

A view down the High Street, c. 1900, taking in the hair cutting rooms of Adrian Francis, with Cox & Sons, gun makers, above; the *Hampshire Advertiser* building; St Lawrence church (demolished 1925) and the Dolphin Hotel, happily still gracing the much-changed scene. Opposite, the 'Short's' sign identifies dispensers of wines and spirits, with the Swiss Restaurant nearby.

Bernard Street, *c.* 1914. Ladders and supporting timbers show work in hand on the south side, flanking a butcher's shop (with carcasses on pavement display), wine and spirit merchants, furniture store, Olivers the boot and shoe makers and Bartram's dinning rooms offering a three course luncheon for a shilling (5p).

Looking along Oxford Street in the 1890s, between the Grapes and Oxford hotels, are the premises of John Mills & Sons, dyers, the Oxford Shipping Stores and several temperance hotels. At the residential end near Orchard Place, No. 61 was the home and surgery of Dr Robert William Foster Welch, whose wife Lucia became Southampton's first woman mayor in 1927.

Horse cabs line Canute Road in the 1890s, waiting for custom from the South Western Hotel and the railway station. In the foreground, east of St Lawrence Road, are the office block styled South Western Chambers and the Ship Tavern, flanked by the split premises of Miller & Sons, naval tailors, hosiers and outfitters.

A popular resort from the 1850s, the Canute Castle Hotel still dominates the Canute Road/Royal Crescent Road corner a century after this photograph was taken. A plaque confidently proclaims 'Near this spot AD 1028 Canute reproved his courtiers.' Who can say?

Around 1900 the Royal Mail Steam Packet Company had its offices at 7-8 Canute Road; the neat plain frontage offset the adjoining premises, covered with advertising for the services of C. Godden & Sons, ship chandlers.

The hotel established by George Radley in the 1840s continued under family management until 1907, when the impressive Victorian building fronting Terminus Terrace was acquired by the Royal Mail Co., and adapted as its Southampton headquarters.

The Clock Tower now at Bitterne Park Triangle was relocated there in 1934, removed to ease traffic at the junction of New Road and Above Bar where it was erected in 1899, by bequest of Mrs H.B. Sayers, primarily as drinking fountains for man and beast. It is here seen, *c*. 1925, flanked by a tram and single-decker motor bus, with cyclists weaving their way between them.

Southampton's first purpose-designed public library at the foot of London Road (shown here, *c*. 1916) opened in 1893 to replace a hall in St Mary Street rented from 1889. Superseded at the Civic Centre in 1939, it was bombed in 1940. The site remained vacant for nearly fifty years until used for new offices.

A 1907 picture of Grosvenor House, an imposing town mansion once the home of William C. Westlake. From 1903 is was a private nursing home, run by the redoubtable Miss Mocatta until the late 1920s, when it closed and the east side of Grosvenor Square was redeveloped.

A view, c. 1920, up London Road, to Carlton Crescent on the left. Dominating the shops are the spires of St Paul's, built in 1828 (the first church serving the suburbs north of the old town) and bombed in 1940. Opposite can be seen the canopy of the former Carlton cinema (1914-22).

Bevois Mount House, Southampton

Photographs of 1905 and 1922 highlight the former elegance of Bevois Mount House and its decline into dilapidation and demolition. Sited within modern Lodge / Cambridge / Avenue / Cedar Roads, it was the centrepiece of the estate developed from 1723 by the third Earl of Peterborough. In the 1840s William Betts financed the improvement and enlargement of the mansion by beginning the process of selling off its 103 acre grounds for smaller-scale housing. From 1896 the house was a private school for young ladies, then a hostel for Hartley College students from 1900. After wartime duty as a transit prison camp for German officers (see p 114) its last role was as part of the Borough Motor Works.

Photographed 111 or more years ago, Red Lodge toll gate stood in Bassett Avenue by what is now Holly Hill, then Rogers nursery gardens. From 1758 two turnpike trusts maintained the Southampton-Winchester road, divided into north and south sections, until taken over by public highway authorities in 1875 and 1886, respectively.

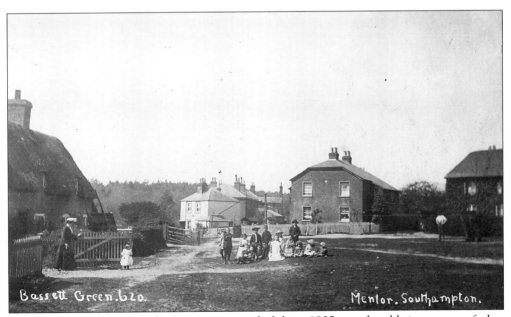

Bassett Green, depicted on this Mentor postcard of about 1905, was the old-time centre of what guidebooks then called 'a pleasant village 2 miles from Southampton.'

A cart stopped for horse refreshment, *c.* 1908, at the Queen Victoria Jubilee memorial fountain and trough, in its original position on the west side of Shirley High Street, outside the Salisbury Arms. It was moved across the road in 1923 and in 1976, after impact repairs, re-erected in the modern shopping precinct.

A busy scene in Hill Lane, *c.* 1905, as milk carts gather at Alfred Brown's Hill Farm Dairy (depicted on a postcard produced for it by F.G.O. Stuart). Brown merged with Harrison in 1940, to be taken over by South Coast Dairies in 1957. After later changes of control, the depot closed for redevelopment of the site in the 1990s, with new houses given the address of Hill Farm Road.

Four Posts has lost its identity through road works and redevelopment but when Herbert Willsteed photographed these cottages, about 1906, they were part of the old hamlet centred around the junction of Hill Lane and Commercial Road, named from the posts carrying direction vanes at the former borough boundary.

Another Willsteed postcard recorded this tranquil scene at Redbridge, *c.* 1908. Local children occupied the road, undisturbed by traffic, although Redbridge was no backwater, being on the Southampton road, with its coastal shipping quay, railway station and track maintenance works (opened 1879, closed 1989).

Deceptively traffic-free, *c.* 1912, is the junction of Bursledon Road and Bitterne Road (part of which through Bitterne village was then styled High Street). Strategically sited between these roads, the Red Lion inn, dating from 1839, still exists but its surroundings were totally transformed in the 1980s.

Local photographer J.T. Eltringham captured this Edwardian scene in Portsmouth Road, Woolston, centred on St Mary's Presbyterian church (replaced by a supermarket) and shops including the Cox family butcher's business (established 1850) that gave its name to the lane running alongside its premises.

Two
Transport and Travel

Although undertaken by separate companies, the railway and docks developments started in the 1830s were recognised from the outset as interdependent, generating traffic to mutual benefit and promoting the growth of Southampton as a major passenger port. More generally, the expanding railway network offered wider possibilities of travel, for pleasure as well as business, and greater economic opportunities for ordinary people to become 'upwardly mobile', as we would say now.

The London & South Western Railway Co. line to London, completed in 1840, sited its Southampton terminus east of the old town, in an area then still semi-rural but well placed in relation to the docks already under construction.

This contemporary engraving depicts the Terminus Station, handsomely designed by Sir William Tite. Eventually closed in 1966, it is 'listed' and preserved as one of the oldest and best of its kind, although now used for a very different purpose.

Southampton West station was built in 1895 to replace the original Blechynden/West End station situated nearer the tunnel. Enlarged in 1934-35, it was then renamed Southampton Central, becoming simply Southampton in 1967, after extensive rebuilding involving the loss of the familiar clock tower.

A view of Southampton West platforms and trains, issued as a postcard by Herbert Willsteed, c. 1908.

Swaythling station, *c.* 1908. Built in 1883, ahead of housing development in the area it served, this exemplifies the suburban stations with which Southampton is still well provided, although they never seem to have been fully used.

Swaythling station (the LSWR established this spelling in place of the earlier Swathling) presented a deceptively domestic appearance in this photograph for a postcard from Mentor & Co., *c.* 1905.

Between shunting duties in the Docks on a day in August 1903, locomotives *Honfleur*, *Granville* and *Alderney*, named on the same pattern of cross-Channel associations as a dozen others dating from the 1890s. *Honfleur* was eventually sold out of BR service in 1949 for work on open-cast coal sites in Wales, until scrapped in 1957.

LSWR locomotive 463 leaving Southampton West on 15 April 1922. Built in 1916, it was the first of a class of ten, mainly used for Waterloo expresses. After experimental conversion to oil burning in 1948, it was scrapped in 1951.

Private omnibuses connecting hotels, stations and docks from the 1840s were superseded in 1879 by the horse-drawn trams of the Southampton Tramways Company. Waiting to leave Oxford Street, *c.* 1895, is No. 22: its signboard reads, 'Shirley, Portswood and Railway Station'.

A busy scene on a fine day, *c.* 1897, (most passengers opt for the open top decks) at the Commercial Road / Above Bar junction of the lines to Shirley and the town centre. The northward expansion of the main shopping thoroughfare is highlighted by the conversion of Prospect House from fashionable residence to provision stores.

Southampton Borough Council bought out the local electricity company in 1896 and in 1898 acquired the Tramways Company, whose lines it then electrified and extended. Corporation VIPs are here seen at the laying of feeder cables in 1899 across Above Bar by Sussex Place.

Civic dignitaries aboard the decorated tram which inaugurated the Shirley-Prospect Place service on 22 January 1900. On the platform, wearing a top hat, is Alderman Dunsford, chairman of the Tramways Committee, who briefly drove the tram on this and similar ceremonial occasions.

Police-operated Stop/Clear signs which regulated the single line passage of trams through the Bargate. The no. 6 for Holy Road in 1914 seems to be empty but passengers were always strictly warned to remain seated on the 'knife board' benching of the open upper decks.

Locally designed low-built tramcars with domed roofs were introduced in 1923. Congestion at the Bargate was later eased by demolition of adjoining properties and parts of the old walls to create a traffic circus around it. The eastern roadway was opened in 1932, as seen here; the western side was completed in 1938.

Steam trains and electric trams promoted suburban growth and increased mobility for both work and pleasure but horse transport was only slowly superseded by motor vehicles. Typical of many such delivery vans in Edwardian times is this one of Lankester & Crook Ltd, the Woolston-based County Supply Stores.

Corporation departments were proud of their well-kept draught horses; some of them are shown on parade on the Common for a special occasion, *c.* 1900.

Combined horsepower, outside the Supermarine works at Woolston: Hubert Scott-Paine's racing motor-boat *Tiddlywinks*, built there in 1919, probably using a redundant flying boat hull.

Representative of steam power on Edwardian roads, this heavy service wagon of about 1905 (registration No. AA 5356) delivered house coal for Southampton Co-operative Society.

One of the first six Thornycroft motor buses introduced by Southampton Corporation Tramways in 1919. This one ran a short-lived service between the Floating Bridge and Tanners Brook, then the borough boundary. Omnibuses offered more flexible and longer routes than the trams but did not totally replace them until 31 December 1949.

The open-top charabanc taking this sober-suited men's outing to Cheddar, *c*. 1920, was operated by the Tourist Motor Co. Started by Bertie Ransom in 1919, it expanded to a fleet of fifty coaches by 1935, when it was taken over by Hants & Dorset Motor Services.

This single-decker, decorated for the 1925 Romsey Carnival, was one of the first ten Leyland vehicles brought into service in 1920, the year the Hants & Dorset title was adopted by the company established in 1917 by William Graham and Walter French.

From 1934 the Corporation Tramways had a maritime division, running the floating bridges across the Itchen after the Council had bought up the company which pioneered these steam-driven chain-operated ferries back in 1836. The system lasted until the City-financed high level toll bridge was opened in 1977.

Fixed bridges across the Itchen were vital for the growth of Southampton. The original timber bridge at Northam erected by a locally organised company in 1797-99 was replaced in 1889 by the wrought iron structure shown here. This was acquired in 1929 by the Corporation, which ended tolls and began running buses across it. The modern pre-stressed concrete bridge was opened in 1954.

Seen here packed with Regatta-watchers in 1895, Cobden Bridge was built in 1883 by the National Liberal Land Company to open up its freehold housing estate at Bitterne Park (incorporated into the borough in 1895). The bridge was handed over to the council 'for the free use of the inhabitants for ever'. It was reconstructed in 1926-28 and renovated in 1979-80.

Three
Gateway to the World

From being one of the county's leading ports in medieval times, Southampton declined to merely local significance, until its importance began to revive in line with the growth of the town from the 1750s. With the advent of steamships in the 1820s and vessels of increased size, the natural advantages of a remarkable double tide effect encouraged the development of extensive open docks, the basis for further growth of commercial and passenger shipping activities from the 1840s, leading eventually to Southampton becoming Britain's 'Gateway to the World' in the heyday of great international liners between the wars.

The Harbour Board initially met the need for better landing facilities by building a substantial timber pier, opened on 8 July 1833 by the Duchess of Kent and her daughter Princess Victoria. The Royal Pier shown here, *c.* 1900, was the outcome of major reconstruction and enlargement in the 1890s.

This aerial view, c. 1925, shows the landing stages branching off the pierhead and the ornate pavilion erected in 1894. It was much used for entertainments, while the pier itself was a popular promenade, given a new approach and attractive entrance building in 1927.

A glimpse of small-scale shipping activity at Northam, c. 1905 (from a Willsteed postcard photograph). As well as quays along the Itchen, the Town Quay (flanked by the Royal Pier) continued busy with local and coastal cargo trade.

A general view of the docks, *c.* 1910. Facilities were steadily extended from the 1840s, when the P&O and Royal Mail companies first established themselves at Southampton, soon to be followed by the Union company (merged with the Castle Line in 1899) and German lines.

Four LSWR steamers in the Outer Dock, *c.* 1905. In the left foreground is the long-lasting *South Western* which ran mostly to St Malo, for forty-four years, until torpedoed in 1918.

Highlighting the increasing importance of the port, the Chinese Ambassador and his entourage inspected Southampton in January 1900 on their tour to foster Anglo-Chinese trade. Their visit began with a civic reception and group photograph at the Royal Pier pavilion.

Transfer of White Star services from Liverpool in 1907 made Southampton the country's premier port but an important precedent was set in 1893 when the American Line established its base here. That March a weekly service was inaugurated by the *New York*, a 10,500 ton steel twin screw steamer, British built in 1888, a regular caller until 1923.

The LSWR bought up the Dock Company in 1892 and soon invested heavily in improvements, notably the Prince of Wales and Trafalgar dry docks, opened in 1895 and 1905. Here work is in progress in June 1910 on the large new dock completed in 1911, providing another 3,800 ft of quay to cater for liners of 40,000 tons and over.

The first White Star liner to use the new dock was the *Olympic*; she made her maiden voyage to New York on 14 June 1911, continuing in service until 1935. Her tragic sister ship *Titanic* is here shown at the quayside before leaving on her fatal initial voyage in April 1912.

Representative of the Royal Mail's 130 years association with Southampton is the *Tagus*, 5,500 tons, 1899-1920. Besides regular services to the West Indies, she carried troops to the Boer War and to garrisons around the Empire; in 1914 she became a hospital ship.

RMS *Asturias*, 12,000 tons, ran the Southampton-Buenos Aires service from 1908 until requisitioned in 1914 and converted into a hospital ship, carrying many thousands of wounded en route to Netley. Torpedoed in 1917, beached and later salvaged, she was rebuilt as a cruise liner, *Arcadian* (1923-30).

In 1894 Southampton became the main trooping port for rotating garrisons around the then far-flung Empire. 'HM Transport' vessels were hired from various companies, such as British India, which operated the 9,000 tons sisters *Neuralia* and *Nevasa* (shown here) from 1912 into the 1940s. In 1914-18 Southampton handled 17,186 ships carrying over 8 million personnel and associated equipment, stores and horses, etc.

Sent to his mother by a soldier waiting in a requisitioned hotel to cross to France on 7 August 1914, this card features an 'Off to Canada' scene at the Docks. Third class and steerage passages for emigrants (segregated from the upper decks) were important revenue-earners for all liner operators.

Southampton from a Supermarine Flying Boat, an anonymous aerial view showing the short-lived train ferry in the foreground. A special pier, 100 yards long, with a 40 yard linkspan, served by a railway extension from the West (later Central) station, was built west of the Royal Pier in 1917, to speed transport of military supplies to France. A service to Dieppe began in December 1917, using three purpose-built wagon carriers. For a second route to Cherbourg, operated only from 6 November 1918 to March 1919, the Canadian government made available the Birkenhead-built train ferry *Leonard*, which crossed the Atlantic in 17 days, to become Train Ferry No. 4. This odd-looking girder-framed craft had three parallel wagon tracks, hydraulically adjusted to meet differences of up to 18 ft in water levels.

The linkspan and the first three ferries went to Harwich in 1922 to run a service to Zeebrugge. The ferries came back to Southampton on war duties in 1940-45; two were lost but one survived as the *Essex Ferry* until 1957. Meanwhile, the *Leonard* was converted into an oil carrier, renamed *Limax*, which lasted until 1932. The disused pier was removed in 1929, when reclamation started for the New Docks and Mayflower Park.

As peacetime garrison duties resumed, families of Royal Sussex regulars left for the West Indies on 30 October 1919, aboard HMT *Voronej*. She was one of eleven Russian merchant ships commandeered early in 1918; they were managed by Royal Mail until sold off in 1923.

HMT *Zeppelin* operated out of Southampton in 1919-20. This 14,600 ton liner was launched in June 1914 in the presence of the airship pioneer himself; she was one of several German vessels taken over by the British and used briefly as troopships, still keeping their original names. She was sold on in 1921 and returned to German ownership in 1927, renamed *Dresden*.

Southampton's status as 'Gateway to the World' was further enhanced in 1919 when Cunard's North American services were transferred from Liverpool and Canadian Pacific liners began calling. One of the ships running its service to Quebec from 1922 was the 24,600 ton, oil burning *Empress of Scotland*, until withdrawn in 1930.

An impressive sight from 1924 was a giant liner (here the *Majestic*) elevated above the water in the massive floating dry dock sited off Town Quay, appearing beside the new Harbour Board offices. Less used after the opening of the King George V dry dock in 1933, it was removed to Portsmouth in 1940.

The crowds along the White Star quay photographed on 10 May 1922 from the *Majestic* as she left on her maiden voyage to New York, nearly eight years after her launching, at Hamburg as the *Bismarck*.

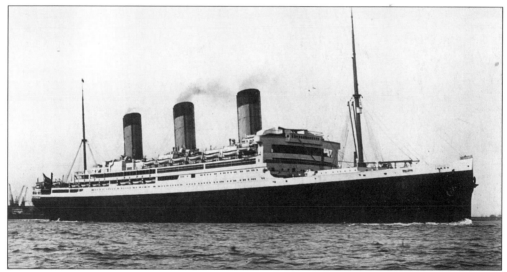

Transferred under reparations arrangements, the *Majestic* was completed and refitted there in 1920-22, to be acclaimed the world's largest ship, at 56,551 tons. Affectionately nicknamed 'Magic Stick', she was a familiar sight at Southampton, making over 200 North Atlantic return trips before being withdrawn in 1936.

The great liners of the inter-war years were indeed 'floating palaces', with luxurious first class cabins and ornately elegant public rooms, such as the 'Palm Court' on the *Majestic*.

The *Leviathan* (originally the *Vaterland*, taken as an American war prize) was publicised by the United States Lines as 'the world's greatest liner' but her 1923-34 North Atlantic career was not a commercial success. The plane being lifted on or off the *Leviathan*, *c.* 1925, may have expedited mail to ports ahead of the liner's arrival but there was then no thought that aviation itself might supersede ocean passenger liners.

'Aerial view of Southampton Docks showing nine of the world's largest liners, gross tonnage 316,000 tons'. On this celebrated Hoffmann postcard, reproducing a photograph taken in November 1931, their names and tonnage are all neatly recorded; from left to right they are: *Empress of Australia*, *Aquitania*, *Majestic*, *Mauretania*, *Berengaria*, *Homeric*, *Arandora Star*, *Alcatara* and *Empress of Britain*.

In 1936 the *Queen Mary*, greatest of the great liners, was hailed as a symbol of national optimism and achievement, with which many were proud to be associated. Here Joseph Rank Ltd of Solent Flour Mills publicise 'Britain's largest millers deliver flour to Britain's largest ship'.

The first notable production from the Supermarine works at Woolston, established by Noel Pemberton Billing in 1913, was PB9, a land-based light biplane for military purposes. This 'Seven Day Bus', constructed in a week following the outbreak of war, made its first 75 mph flight from a field at Netley on 11 August 1914. Works manager Hubert Scott-Paine is at the right of the group by the plane.

Supermarine became famous for its flying boats, designed by R.J. Mitchell, firstly for military, then for civilian use and speed racing. This Sea Eagle, at Woolston marine airport in 1924, operated Imperial Airways services to France and the Channel Islands. It carried six passengers in the enclosed bow; behind it, the pilot occupied an open cockpit.

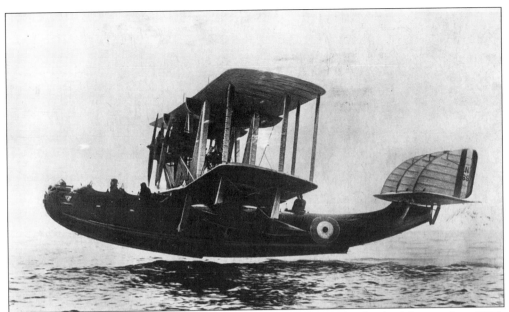

Supermarine 'Southampton' twin engine flying boats were built for the Air Ministry from 1925. Initially wooden hulled, they soon pioneered metal construction. In 1927 four of them made remarkable 27,000 mile flights to the Far East and Australia.

DESIGNED AND CONSTRUCTED BY
THE SUPERMARINE AVIATION WORKS LTD.
PROPRIETORS VICKERS (AVIATION) LIMITED.

Sea planes designed by R.J. Mitchell won the Schneider Trophy for the third time in 1929, when this S.6 set new records of over 300 mph. Outright victory in 1931 and further developments led to production from 1936 of the famous 'Spitfire' fighters.

A 1938 scene at the New Docks: dwarfed by the Cunard liner *Berengaria* is Short S23 flying boat *Coolangatta*, one of those operating the Imperial Airways Empire Airmail services introduced in 1937.

G-ADHJ in the foreground of the previous picture was the seaplane 'Mercury', here seen mounted on the flying boat 'Maia' to form a novel pick-a-back composite aircraft, from which the smaller mail-carrying plane was launched in mid air.

Four

Events and Occasions

Edwardian newspapers contained few topical illustrations. To fill this gap, enterprising photographers offered postcards of local events and occasions. One of the earliest was this anonymous production of Saturday 14 March 1903, postmarked 11 pm and annotated, 'this is a snapshot of Joe Chamberlain taken this morning'. Returning from a four-month visit to South Africa to promote reconciliation and unity, the Colonial Secretary was accorded an enthusiastic reception. He landed from the steamer Norman at 9 am, was driven with the Mayor in an open carriage to the Hartley Institute for a civic welcome, and thence to the West station to take the 10.45 train to London.

The Mayor (Richard Andrews) and Corporation officials leaving the liner *Carisbrooke Castle* early on Saturday 13 April 1907, after welcoming General Botha, the Premier of Transvaal, who had come to attend the conference of Colonial Premiers in London.

Stephen Cribb of Portsmouth again brought his camera to Southampton Docks on 27 April 1910, to record the return of Lord Kitchener, from India and Australia via America, aboard the White Star liner, *Oceanic*. On his previous visit, in July 1902, Lord Kitchener had been made a Freeman of the Borough.

'Celebrating St George's Day at Southampton'. This Stuart view of the crowd watching a military parade, *c.* 1905, on the West Marlands (used for building the Civic Centre in the 1930s) exemplifies the uncomplicated patriotism and national confidence widespread before the First World War.

On Empire Day, 24 May, popular pride in Britain's imperial status found expression in church services, parades and processions, leading to gatherings such as this at Bitterne Park Triangle in 1911, recalled by an anonymous souvenir postcard.

On the morning of Friday 20 May 1911, the day of national funeral ceremonies for King Edward VII, the Mayor and Corporation went in procession to St Mary's for a civic memorial service. Special services were also held at most other churches.

At 4.30 pm thousands of people left Queen's Park in another procession, joined at the Audit House by civic dignitaries, to the West Marlands, where police, army and other local bands played for a mass open-air service - the subject of postcards issued from the Above Bar studio of Chandler & Co.

MAYOR PLANTING TREES IN WEST PARK
JUNE 22, 1911.

Two plane saplings were planted in West Park on 22 June 1911 as part of the borough's commemoration of the coronation of King George V. The Mayor, Edward Bance, was attending the service in Westminster Abbey: the silver spade was actually wielded by the Mayoress and senior members of the Council.

FEU DE JOIE, CORONATION DAY, SOUTHAMPTON.   3.

Rain later put a damper on other celebrations but thousands braved it to watch sports on the Common and a parade of Territorial Army units, who fired a *feu de joie*, another subject for Chandler postcards.

Thousands gathered at 6 am on May Day to hear St Mary's choir sing hymns and carols from the Bargate roof, an ancient custom revived in 1906 by the Rector, Canon Lovett. In 1911 (above) the police were there to keep the tramway clear but in 1915 (below) the crowd seems to have been allowed to occupy the whole of the road: May Day celebrations were evidently unaffected by the war.

Sizeable crowds also made their way to the Common, where this photograph was taken at 6.30 am. Females predominated, some sporting floral bonnets. Did the girls follow the old custom of bathing their faces in the dew, believed to enhance their beauty?

Thousands (mainly men) used to throng the High Street, around Holy Rood church, to welcome in the New Year. This was the scene on New Year's Eve 1913, caught in a flashlight photograph by Adolphe Rapp of Bernard Street.

Disasters could be photogenic! Someone from the Oxford Street studio of Mallett & Sons was quickly on the scene after the billiard hall of the Northam Conservative Club was destroyed by a gas explosion on 1 May 1905.

Over £20,000 damage was caused by the great fire which on the evening of 3 January 1912 gutted Hart's Domestic Bazaar and Furniture Emporium in Bridge Street (later incorporated into Bernard Street).

A horse-drawn lifeboat negotiates the turn from High Street into East Street during a demonstration parade in 1906.

More functional were the smaller boats rowed along Northam streets (like this one snapped outside the Coopers Arms at the corner of Millbank and William Streets) on Boxing Day 1912, when high tide, heavy rain and fierce gales combined to cause severe flooding, affecting over a thousand houses.

The heavy snowstorm which unexpectedly covered the area in the early hours of 25 April 1908 briefly brought the town to a virtual standstill. Several enterprising photographers set out to record the unseasonable snow scenes, such as this one on the Western Esplanade, for topical postcard sales.

Many such cards are still around but rarely seen is this one, 'The Morning Post', depicting one of the stalwart postmen who braved difficult conditions to undertake their delivery rounds.

Since 1913 the Western Esplanade has been dominated by the 50 ft column commemorating the 1620 sailing of the Pilgrim Fathers in the *Mayflower*. An unknown postcard photographer caught the moment on the afternoon of 15 August 1913 as canvas screens slid down to unveil it. Instead of cutting the cord to release them, the US Ambassador, Dr Walter Hines Page, used a silver 'torch of liberty' to burn through it. Descendants of original *Mayflower* settlers unveiled family memorial panels, watched by thousands, including Professor F.J.C. Hearnshaw, the historian who had returned to see the culmination of the project he had initiated.

Southampton, of course, had special reasons to mark its *Mayflower* connection, for it was from its West Quay that the vessel had sailed on 15 August 1620. Her better known association with Plymouth as the final port of departure a month later was incidental and accidental, arising from the need to repair the accompanying *Speedwell*, which had to be given up and sold off there.

Southampton's memorial was inaugurated on 15 August 1911 but subscriptions failed to raise the £2,000 needed for a design representing the *Mayflower*'s bow projecting over the water's edge. The committee then had to settle for the simpler, but still impressive, column of Portland stone, prepared and carved in the workshops of Messrs Garret & Haysom, at a cost of some £500.

1226 FUNERAL OF THE LATE P.C. RICHARDS H.C. WOOLSTON. SEPT 6-1911

Fireman, policemen and local councillors headed the procession to Jesus Chapel, Pear Tree Green, on 6 September 1911 for the funeral of PC Harry Richards, a popular Woolston constable whose life was cut short by illness at thirty-two.

Among other postcards produced by local photographer James Eltringham was this souvenir of the Fancy Dress New Year's Party of the Woolston Cooperative Junior Guild, enjoyed by some 150 children in the Oswald Hall, Portsmouth Road, on the evening of 7 January 1913.

Five
People Who Served

Before and between the wars, many small shops and businesses competed to meet local needs for goods and services of all kinds. From small beginnings, some family enterprises flourished into large-scale or long-lasting establishments. Successful Victorian businessmen often undertook public service, through the borough council and voluntary organisations.

On the then outskirts of the town, at the corner of Romsey Road and Redbridge Hill, stood the old-fashioned shop of Harry Froud, grocer, pork butcher and poulterer. He was photographed outside it in 1905 (with his grand-daughter?) and may have died soon after as Mrs Alice Froud (his widow?) is recorded as running the shop for twenty years until 1926, when Miss Nellie Froud took over. It gave way to road widening after 1930.

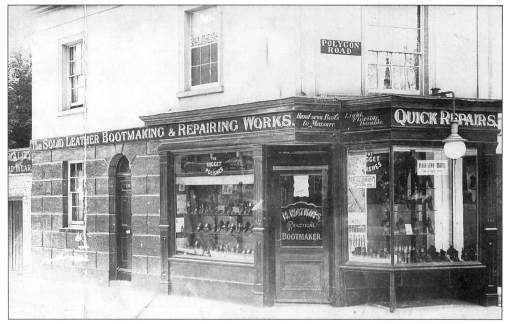

Evocative of old-time craftsmanship, the 'Solid Leather Bootmaking and Repairing Works' offering 'light, flexible, durable handsewn boots to measure' was established in 1898 by Henry Watkins at 82 Bedford Place and continued by his son William into the 1920s. On the corner of the part of Polygon Road renamed Henstead Road in 1921, the building is now a video shop.

Jim Mitchell stands by the door of the little general shop he ran from about 1923 at 3 Southbrook Road, at the west end of Blechynden Terrace by the Central Station forecourt. He moved about 1935 to a house in Central Station Road and when this was bombed in 1940 he resumed business at another shop in Western Espanade, continuing there until about 1960.

John Wickham took over the shop at 39 London Road in 1904 and for the next ten years traded as 'furnishing draper, blind maker and bedding manufacturer'. He was evidently a go-ahead man, quickly installing a telephone (No. 44x) and issuing this publicity postcard showing the dapper draper between his well-filled shop windows.

At 65 London Road, c. 1910, students and staff of the local branch of Skerry's Civil Service and Commercial College posed on the balcony above the shop and crowded forecourt of William Dibben, gas and water fitter and electrical engineer.

Bert Olding drives the horse and cart delivering fruit and vegetables for John Barnes, market gardener of Broadlands Road, Old Portswood, *c.* 1910.

Posing by one of its wagons, *c.* 1920, four employees of Frederick Smith & Sons, furniture removers and storage contractors, a firm established in 1879, with premises in Compton Walk from 1915 to the 1950s.

Founded in 1887 by a small group of young dock workers, Southampton Co-operative Society flourished steadily; it established its central stores in St Mary's Road in 1907, complemented by several neighbourhood shops, like this one at the corner of Earls Road and Avenue Road, where staff lined up for the camera, *c.* 1910.

Another Co-op postcard of 1910 featured the Society's steam bakery, situated in Trinity Road, near Six Dials: three bakers posed by the ovens and a large tray of double-decker cottage loaves.

This advertising card for the 'electric motor flag factory' of S.W. Wolff & Co., 75-76 High Street, was produced in 1910. Mrs Sophia Wolff was first recorded as a High Street flag maker in 1847; the family business survived the blitzing of its premises in 1940 and continued elsewhere into the 1970s.

The years 1910-14 were marked by bitter industrial and political disputes. In 1911 Southampton strikes involved bakers, plumbers and other groups as well as shipping and dock workers. This large and respectable demonstration marching from the Terminus Station is headed by the banner of the National Union of GasWorkers and General Labourers.

Retired headmaster Richard Kimber established the brickworks at Highfield where this photograph was taken, *c.* 1910. The business was continued by his son, Alderman Sir Sidney Kimber. The old brickfield extended west of University Road to the Common, later providing an attractive site for the University buildings.

Workers of George Blake, 'The Better Builder, specialist in small deposit house purchase', photographed on 20 March 1928 outside houses they had built in Downs Park Crescent, Totton. These and others in nearby roads were followed by hundreds more (all costing under £500) across the Maybush Triangle, brought within the borough in 1954.

George Simon Brinton, who died in 1868 at the early age of 46, put his name on the street scene. Greatly extending his father's business, he built many hundreds of houses in Newtown, St Mary's and elsewhere, notably East Park Terrace, which included one as his own home. A Liberal town councillor from 1850, as Mayor in 1864 he there entertained the Italian patriot leader Garibaldi at the start of his triumphal visit to England – as recalled by the plaque now at Tudor House museum.

It was presented by Edwin Jones & Co. in 1942 when 'Garibaldi House' was demolished after bomb damage. Following various changes of ownership and use (in the early 1900s as a College for Young Ladies, then a private hotel), 27 East Park Terrace was bought in 1911 by the department store to serve as a staff social club and hostel.

Photographed in 1880, Edwin Jones (1832-96) came from Romsey in 1860 to open a small drapery shop in East Street. He quickly developed an extensive business, constantly enlarging his premises and diversifying his trade, including wholesale from 1880. He held strong religious, humanitarian and Liberal convictions, applied as an enlightened employer and in public service, as a councillor, twice Mayor in the 1870s, and Parliamentary candidate (unsuccessful).

Subject of a 1903 Cosser postcard, the imposing late Victorian department store facing the Parks was styled Queen's Buildings. It was modernised in the early 1930s, bombed in 1940 and rebuilt in the late 1950s. In 1928 Edwin Jones & Co. Ltd. became part of the Debenhams group; it ceased using the founder's name in 1973 but older customers still talk of Edwin Jones.

This Stuart postcard was used in 1904 by a descendant of Richard Andrews, subject of the hugely ornate 1861 memorial in East Park. Southampton's own Victorian 'Dick Whittington', Andrews (1798-1859) rose from poor farm boy to prosperous coach builder in Above Bar. A staunch Liberal, he served as mayor five times in the 1850s. The lofty pedestal, elaborately carved by Philip Brannon in soft Bath stone, weathered badly and was dismantled in 1971; now remounted on a squat cylinder, the Andrews statue is no longer impressive.

Another strong Liberal who served Southampton well was Edward Bance (1842-1925, portrayed here at 38); he did well as surveyor, valuer, estate agent and auctioneer and was for forty years prominent as a Volunteer officer (prime mover in the building of the Drill Hall in St Mary Street) and in civic affairs. Thrice mayor, he was instrumental in getting the Council to buy Tudor House, opened in 1912 as the town's first museum.

Recorded by the camera of Thomas Hibberd James, *c.* 1895, the bookshop of Henry March Gilbert (1845-1931) was then well established at 26 Above Bar. It is now part of Marks and Spencer's site. The firm of H.M. Gilbert & Sons has since flourished into its fifth generation of family control, still providing knowledgeable personal service and browsing delights in room upon room of new and secondhand books.

Founder Henry Gilbert came from Essex in 1859 to open a shop in Bernard Street. Taken over by his son on his death in 1869, what was already styled 'Ye Olde Booke Shoppe' was briefly transferred, around 1875, to 103 High Street before settling in Above Bar for over sixty years. H.M. Gilbert (1845-1931) was bibliophile and publisher as well as bookseller; he issued his own pioneering Hampshire bibliographies and the *History of Southampton* by Revd J.S. Davies (1883), also the *Transactions of the Hampshire Field Club*. H.M.G. made time for public service in municipal affairs and as a prominent Free Church office-holder. In 1895 he opened a branch shop at Winchester, moved in 1904 to the historic building in The Square, still in use. His son Owen Gilbert (1875-1953) continued the business through half a century, moving the Southampton shop in 1939 to its present premises in Portland Street, oddly numbered $2\frac{1}{2}$. On his return in 1946 from six years war service as a fighter pilot, Bruce Gilbert succeeded his father. Since his death in 1991 the family business has been continued by his son Richard, now looking ahead to celebrating its 150th anniversary!

Southampton's Old Veteran Wishes You A Happy. Prosperous and Peaceful New Year

His Motto —
There will always be "An England."

William Burrough Hill in his 95th year 1940

William Burrough Hill sent 1940 New Year greetings in his own firm hand, with a photograph of himself at his desk in his den at Bridell Lodge, Regents Park. Then in his 95th year (he lived to his 97th, dying on 27 May 1941), he displayed a remarkable talent for minuscule penmanship, e.g. writing the Lord's Prayer three times within the area of a threepenny piece. Southampton's 'Grand Old Man' contributed significantly to the business and public life of the town. As surveyor, estate agent and auctioneer, he had many interests, including housing developments in the suburbs. He cherished a love of old Southampton and formed a large collection of works of art illustrating its history; he sold it to the Corporation in 1910.

W.B. Hill is now chiefly remembered in connection with Stag Gates, the stone pillars at the entrance to Bevois Mount House (page 18). Having acquired their site, he used them as a private bill-posting station and tried unsuccessfully to sell them to the Council for widening Lodge Road. In 1919 he made them a conditional gift, which resulted in disposal of the stonework, for £15, to be used for flower boxes in East Park, and retention of the stags, which he removed and later buried in his garden. The full story, separating fact and myth, is told in the writer's article in *Hampshire* magazine, November 1996.

Six

Care for Soul,
Body and Mind

In Victorian and Edwardian times, when the pattern of everyday life seemed simpler and more stable, religious beliefs were stronger and involvement with places of worship was more widespread than today. Social activities as well as religious and educational provision centred more on churches and chapels, which were accorded proportionately greater support by their congregations.

The mother church of Southampton is St Mary's. Originally serving the Saxon town of Hamwic, its buildings have a long and chequered history, being several times renewed or altered. The church as enlarged in 1833 soon proved inadequate for the needs of a parish rapidly increasing in population. Complete rebuilding was energetically promoted in the 1870s by the Rector, Canon Wilberforce. The eminent architect G.E. Street was engaged to design the new church, for which the Prince of Wales laid the dedication stone on 12 August 1878. As completed in 1884 (shown here from a Cosser postcard, c. 1902), it still lacked tower and spire, for which funds were not then available.

Tower and spire were eventually added in 1913-14, thanks to the efforts of Canon Neville Lovett, Rector 1912-25, later Bishop of Portsmouth, then Salisbury. The spire, here still surrounded by scaffolding, was completed on 5 January 1914, when Canon Lovett, accompanied by his two young daughters, climbed 200 ft to help place the final stone and cross.

In memory of her husband, Mrs Mary Wingrove gave a set of eight bells. On 1 May 1914 they arrived from Taylor's Loughborough foundry and were drawn in procession from the Docks (Terminus) Station. They were first rung on 20 June. A few years later their sound across the water inspired Douglas Furber to write the song *The Bells of St Mary's*, with the Australian composer A. Emmott Adams.

76

The arrival of Henry VIII and Queen Catherine for one of the ten presentations of the 'Tudor Southampton' pageant, staged in the Deanery grounds in June 1914, written by Canon Lovett to raise the last £1,000 of the £18,000 cost of the tower and spire. St Mary's was bombed in 1940 but these features were reconstructed in 1948 and rebuilding was completed in 1956.

The spire of St Michael's church under repair in 1924. Dating in part from about 1070, it is the city's oldest church, the only medieval one surviving substantially intact. The spire was built in the fifthteenth century, reconstructed in 1732 and extended to its present height of 165 ft in 1877; the upper part was reconstructed in 1968.

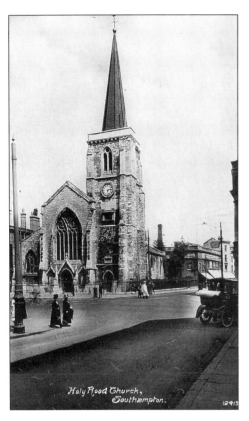

Holy Rood Church,
Southampton.

Seen here in the 1920s, Holy Rood held special place among old Southampton churches as 'the sailors' church' and 'the Mayor's church', with both official and popular celebrations centred on its 'Proclamation porch' and adjoining 'asphalt'. Gutted by bombing in 1940, its ruined shell has, since 1957, served as a Merchant Navy memorial shrine.

HOLYROOD CHURCH SPIR
HEIGHT 4'8"
LENGTH 3'9"
WEIGHT 20½ lbs.

Exemplifying its maritime associations, until lost when the spire crashed in flames on the night of 30 November 1940, this artistic model sailing ship topped the weathervane for some 200 years. It was photographed in the summer of 1907, when taken down for repair and regilding.

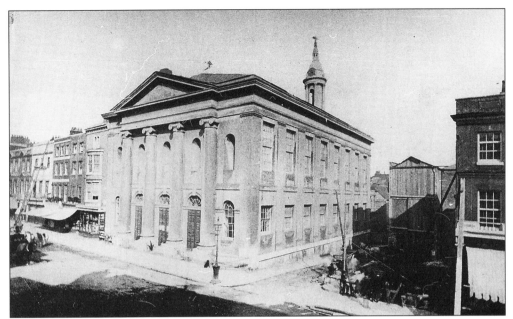

Dominating the High Street, on the north corner of East Street, stood All Saints church, built in 1792-95 to replace a ruinous medieval structure. Designed by Willey Reveley in the style of a Greek temple, it was economically constructed of brick and stucco, later cemented.

The roof (95 x 61 ft) was noteworthy for being 'one of the largest unsupported ceilings in the kingdom'. Both photographs are from about 1900. Following the bombing of the church in 1940 its site was deconsecrated in 1954 and sold for redevelopment.

All Saints served a socially mixed parish in various ways. Its associated Scout Troop, which was noted for its brass band, is here shown as Silver Cup winners in the 1914 County Rally at Bournemouth, under its Scoutmaster Isaac Snook.

This 1903 Cosser postcard gives a seemingly rural, sylvan aspect to St Peter's church, but for the tramlines along Commercial Road! Built in 1846 to serve a distant section of All Saints, which became a separate parish in 1861, St Peter's was redundant in the 1980s, when the building was sold for use as restaurant and coffee bar, etc.

A 1905 view of St Andrew's Presbyterian Church, Brunswick Place, built in 1853 on a site given by Andrew Lamb, superintendent engineer of the P&O Company. The 'Scotch Church' served many employees of this and other shipping companies, shipbuilders and docks contractors etc. Made redundant after a merger with the Avenue United Reform Church, St Andrew's was demolished in the 1990s and replaced by yet another office block.

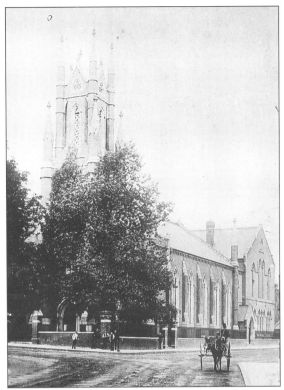

Merger in 1935 with the Avenue Congregational Church (its own 1890s offshoot) ended the separate existence of the Albion Church established in St Mary Street since the 1840s. In April 1909 it held a highly successful four-day 'Indian Empire Bazaar', professionally staged at the Coliseum skating rink in Portland Terrace. (Photographed by 'Max Mills', the business name of Wilfred Ashby, a man of many talents.)

A photogenic subject recorded between the wars, the ivy-clad tower of old Millbrook church was a medieval survival; the rest of the structure was rebuilt in 1827. Superseded by Holy Trinity in 1874 and little used thereafter, the church near the water (dedicated to St Nicholas, patron saint of seafarers) deteriorated until eventually it was demolished in 1939.

The ancient ceremony of blessing the waters was revived on Rogation Sunday 1920. The Mayor and Corporation, consuls and representatives of various churches and maritime organisations went in procession from Holy Rood through the Docks (seen here in front of Harland & Wolff's repair works) to Town Quay, where the Port Chaplain led an open-air service.

In Edwardian times, dogs with collecting boxes on their backs helped gather funds for Railway and Seamen's Orphanages. For the latter, at Tremona Court (hence Tremona Road), 'Nellie Bly' presumably perambulated widely, for hers was the pen-mame of American journalist Elizabeth Cochrane Seaman, author of *Around the World in 72 Days*.

A forerunner of Fred Woolley House, the Home of Recovery opened in 1908 at The Grange, Swaythling, held a fund-raising garden party on 1 September 1909. Its highlight was the play *Jappy Chappy*, directed by Italia Conti. This is one of several postcards produced by W.M. Phillips of Hampton Park.

A contemporary engraving of 'The Grand Masonic Ceremony of Laying the First Stone of the South Hants Infirmary' on 10 July 1843. Doctors John and William Bullar were the prime movers in establishing this hospital at Newtown, then an outer suburb offering fresh country air!

The first of many extensions were the wings and chapel added in the 1850s, completing the frontage along Fanshawe Street (named after Revd Charles Fanshawe, another founder); a Willsteed postcard, c. 1905.

Laying the foundation stone of the 'New Workhouse Infirmary' at Shirley Warren on 6 March 1900. Built by the Guardians of the Poor for the Union of Southampton parishes, it was first styled the Incorporation Infirmary, becoming the Borough Hospital in 1929 (when the Council took over the work of the Guardians) and Southampton General Hospital in 1948 when brought within the NHS.

A 1910 view of the original Infirmary and nurses home (at the right). Daily travel to Shirley Warren would not have been easy in the 1900s but the Guardians had an eye to the future when securing a 35-acre site there.

King Edward VI Grammar School, Southampton.

Founded in 1553, King Edward VI School had a chequered history until re-established in 1860. Subsequent growth led to a move in 1896 from Bugle Street to these handsome new buildings on the Kingsbridge House site and thence, in 1938, to larger modern premises off Hill Lane, since greatly enlarged.

Exercise, Hurst Leigh School, Southampton

Handel College, conducted from 1864 by father and son Aaron and Frank Harvey, occupied from 1897 this large old house at the Polygon (site of Sembal House). It was taken over in 1912 by Lionel Caufeild's Hurst Leigh School, which continued there until 1936 (from a publicity postcard, printed in Germany, *c.* 1913).

Standard V of 1905 at St Denys typifies thousands of similar classes in the public elementary schools provided by the School Board form the 1870s. St Denys School was well built in 1881-82; recently refurbished, it still serves the local community.

So also do those parts of the 1889-1900 Board Schools at Northam which survived the war. In May 1913 pupils joined in the *entente cordiale* celebrations during a busy visit by a large party from Le Harve, returning a Southampton civic visit there in 1912.

The Sisters of La Sainte Union bought the old house in the Avenue called Archers Lodge and in 1881 there opened 'a superior school for young ladies' which developed as the Convent High School until merged with St Anne's in 1963-73.

St Anne's, a secondary day school opened in 1904, was soon established in its own building off Carlton Crescent, seen here in 1922. Along with the original Convent H.S. premises, they were destroyed by bombing in 1940.

Presenting their first entertainment are students of the original 1904 intake to the residential training college for women teachers founded by Mother Antonia on the Avenue campus of La Sainte Union. More recently, it has expanded and diversified as LSU College of Higher Education.

Initiating Council provision of selective secondary education for girls, the Girls' Grammar School was opened in 1907 in new buildings at Argyle Road. Shown here are some of the girls in the long narrow playground, formerly a ropewalk. The school moved to Hill Lane in 1936.

Hartley University College occupied this High Street building erected in 1862, applying the balance of the disputed bequest of Henry Robinson Hartley. The move to new accommodation at Highfield planned for 1914 was delayed until 1919 by use as a military hospital (page 111). The vacated premises in the High Street were eventually sold for demolition and redevelopment in 1936.

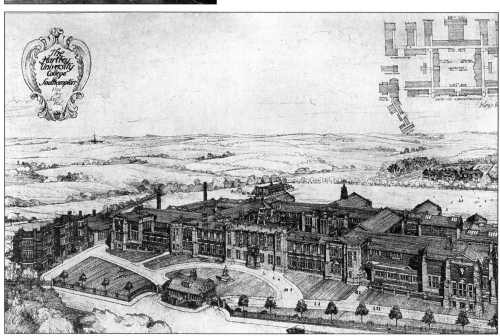

This postcard, c. 1912, publicised the architects' plan and drawing of the buildings ambitiously proposed for the Highfield site. Only the first phase could then be afforded. Large-scale expansion had to await the achievement of University status in 1952.

Seven
Leisure and Pleasure

Before the extension of mass entertainment, spectator sport and tourism industries and at a time when few workers enjoyed paid holidays, people in the early part of this century were more actively involved in arranging their own less sophisticated forms of recreation, which often centred on church, public house or place of work.

Reflecting the more rigid class distinctions of those times with the 1st, 2nd and 3rd Class Bars and what proprieter Charlie Kimber called 'Kim's Kosy Korner', the Pembroke Hotel stood in a little square east of the Bargate, cleared away for road works in 1930.

Day outings to seaside or New Forest were often men-only rather than family affairs. All soberly dressed, this group posed beside the horse-drawn brakes before leaving the Cliff Hotel at Woolston, *c*. 1905.

Flanked by their coachman, the jaunty 'Star Tap Boys', from the Star Hotel in the High Street, were enjoying their outing to the New Forest on a summer Sunday in 1905, an occasion meriting another souvenir postcard.

This fine body of sober-suited men photographed by J.T. Eltringham were the employees of Dixon Bros & Hutchinson enjoying their works outing on Saturday 15 July 1905 at Crabwood (then a country house, now part of the Ordnance Survey premises). The firm was then recently established at Wharf Road, Woolston as 'manufacturers of motor cars and motor boats'; it continued there for some twenty years.

The Southampton branch of the UK Railway Temperance Union, one of several such organisations, publicised its message of total abstinence - 'our drink is water, God's gift to man' - with this tableau on a horse wagon, c. 1910.

For open air recreation and enjoyment, the Common was a great amenity for large families from small houses in the closely built older parts of the town. Vast crowds were drawn to Bank Holiday fairs, whose carousel attractions included George Baker's 'Traction Centre Gallopers', photographed in about 1905.

Rides on Ninehams pony carts were a popular feature of the fairs - at least for the children whose parents were able to afford them. This was photographed by Brain of Shirley, *c*. 1910.

An Edwardian vista along the tree-canopied Lover's Walk, which was probably the most permanently popular feature of the Common for romantic perambulations.

The Cowherds has been refurbished several times but still retains most of its original appearance, as built in 1762, primarily as an inn rather than for the old-time town official overseeing cattle pastured on the Common. In the early 1900s the tenant was also a horse dealer who offered 'private landaus and cabs for hire' and kept 'livery and bait stables'.

The refreshment pavilion on the Common seems a mundane feature for Mr Brain's postcard photograph, *c.* 1910, but this temporary wooden building held contentious topicality as the subject of a mini-saga of narrowly divided Council votes extending through the years 1909-12.

Originally erected as the secretary's office for the Royal Counties Agricultural Show earlier in 1908, it was that summer bought by the Council (for £50) as an immediately available cheap precursor of a proposed Temperance Refreshment Pavilion/Tea House. Catering contractor Joseph Joyce secured the lease of it but soon there were petitions, letters and Council motions demanding its removal, as an illegal structure on the Common. It was retained until after the Coronation festivities but in October 1911 the Council accepted Joyce's tender of £25 to dismantle and remove it.

Meanwhile the Council offered premiums of £10 and £5 for schemes from local architects for a new tea house; it found that acceptable designs could not be realised within the £500 cost limit previously set. Two successive Council votes in December 1911/January 1912 against/for any further action contradicted each other by majorities of 1 and 2 and the erection of a permanent tea house was then deferred until 1915 – by which time this storm in a tea cup had been overtaken by the outbreak of war and use of large areas of the Common for military camps.

Before and after the First World War, the Territorial Army and other uniformed brass bands were engaged by the Corporation to give popular concerts, both on the Common and in Palmerston Park, where a bandstand was erected in 1885. Sited between the statue and New Road, as shown here, c. 1910, this cast iron structure probably disappeared in 1940, through bomb damage and/or salvage for the war effort.

The Southampton Post Office Band, winners of trophies in regional competitions held at Marlborough and Shanklin in 1909-11, posed with them for F.G.O. Stuart to produce postcard souvenirs.

Exemplifying bands and concert parties formed by ships' crews is this group aboard the *Sarnia*, a 1,500 ton LSWR passenger steamer running Channel Islands services from April 1911. Taken in 1914 for duty as an armed boarding vessel, she was torpedoed and sunk in the Mediterranean on 12 September 1918.

Offically opened by the Mayor on 12 January 1910, the roller skating rink in Shirley Road (north corner of Janson Road) claimed to be 'the largest and best appointed in Hampshire'. In November 1914 it was taken over to accommodate German prisoners of war. Its post-war reopening proved unsuccessful and after a few years use for miscellaneous entertainments the building (basically corrugated iron) was demolished for 'redevelopment'.

In 1890 the Corporation took over the sea water baths on the Western Esplanande, run since 1854 by a private company, and in 1892-4 opened new buildings providing covered baths, washing and laundry facilities and Turkish baths.

This 'aerial' view of the open air pool (on reclaimed land, between the later Pirelli and Toys Я Us sites) was probably photographed by F.G.O. Stuart from the chimney of the nearby electricity station under construction in 1903.

The open pool was originally reserved for gentlemen but from the turn of the century it was in demand for swimming galas, like this children's event of 1905, the subject of postcards issued by G. Whitfield Cosser.

Between the wars, while improving housing conditions lessened the need for 'baths for the working classes', attendances at the baths soared to nearly 100,000 in a sunny summer month as people flocked to swim and sunbathe at the 'Lido'. It eventually closed in 1974. The new Central Baths, opened in 1962, provided only indoor baths.

Hartley University College First XI of 1907, smartly turned out for their group photograph; they enjoyed quite a good season ; won 4, drew 3, lost 5.

These more informal cricketers of about 1910 remain anonymous but were presumably an office or business side, rather short of gear but looking highly respectable, with many still wearing ties; they were well enough organised to commission a professional photographer, Adolphe Rapp, in business at 39 Bernard Street, 1908-14.

Mr Rapp found a profitable sideline in producing souvenir postcards for football crowds at the Dell, as at this Southern League match between the Saints and Reading, *c.* 1908. Everyone looks remarkably sombre and sedate, all wearing caps or hats and not a coloured scarf or team favour in sight!

Typifying many amateur sides are the men of Trinity Sports Club, associated with the South Western Hotel, posing with their trophies in 1908.

Members of the Southern Division, St John's Ambulance Brigade, here photographed, *c.* 1905, by J.W. Oakley, assiduously attended football matches, also other sports events and entertainments.

A packed house for the special children's matinee ('the noise was terrific, the laughter wonderful' wrote the sender of the postcard picture) on Wednesday 30 December 1925 at the Hippodrome in Ogle Road. Opened in 1883, it closed in 1939.

Nell Gwynn in November 1932 was one of 104 different plays presented weekly at the Grand Theatre in 1931-33 by Alfred Denville's stock company. Opened in 1898, this 1,800-seat theatre had staged many star productions but from the 1930s audiences declined and it finally closed in 1959.

Among Southampton's many cinemas was the Gaiety at 169 High Street, built in 1914 and here seen showing the 1923 Hollywood film *Truth About Wives*, starring the then popular Betty Blythe. The Gaiety introduced talkies in September 1929, with Al Jolson's *The Singing Fool*, and survived the war, eventually closing in April 1956.

Eight

From War to Peace

Southampton's importance as Britain's premier trooping port, demonstrated by the dispatch of over a million men to the Boer War of 1899-1902, was confirmed by extensive peacetime movements of garrisons around the then far-flung Empire. Presaging the First World War was the embarkation, on Monday 5 September 1904, of 11,439 men and 2,771 horses, from the army units engaged in a large-scale exercise under General Sir John French, simulating an enemy invasion of Essex. The troops had marched from Winchester to camp on the Common, where thousands of townsfolk gathered on Sunday to watch church parades and enjoy band concerts. Max Mills (Wilfred Ashby) was busy snapping scenes like this one (below) for his topical postcards.

One of a number of postcards produced by J.W. Oakley showing troopships leaving the docks in Edwardian times, taking garrison forces to India and elsewhere.

The Baggage Guard of the Royal Garrison Artillery marching along the Royal Pier on Saturday afternoon 29 May 1909 to embark on the *Prince of Wales* to the Isle of Wight for the annual fortnight training camp.

Ten RGA companies and various other volunteer units had their headquarters at the Territorial Army drill hall in St Mary's Road. Dated 1889, this building is now used as a leisure centre.

The Drill Hall was earlier made available for other purposes, as in 1910 for this flower show; the floral displays are incongruously flanked by large field guns.

REST CAMP SOUTHAMPTON

Photographed under construction in August 1914, some of the wooden huts erected on the Common; supplemented by numerous tents, they formed the Rest (ie. transit) Camp, primarily as overnight accommodation for troops *en route* to the docks. During the First World War over 8 million servicemen embarked from Southampton.

Within the Rest Camp, the St John's Ambulance refreshment hut was a popular place for soldiers. Here volunteer helpers pose behind the counter, prior to opening for the rush of customers.

Then living in Archers Road, A.G. Steavenson was handily placed to record horse artillery proceding down the Avenue to the docks in August 1914 (above) and likewise infantry on the march there in October (below). Returning from his own overseas service, 'Steavie' became a distinguished geologist and respected Labour Party stalwart, whose manifold public service to Southampton was recognised by the CBE he was awarded in 1965.

For five years the Avenue Congregational Church maintained its Soldiers Rest Hall (in the original 'tin church'), providing refreshments, recreational and writing facilities used daily by thousands more than the few posing for this postcard photograph. Church workers also developed a splendid system for serving troops on the march down the Avenue.

Staff of No. 9 Ambulance Train, Southampton Docks. 11th Aug., 1916.

Photographed on 11 August 1916, are the staff of No. 9 Ambulance Train, one of twenty taking casualties to Netley and other hospitals. Altogether, some 2.6 million war wounded were brought back to Britain, half of them via Southampton.

In August 1914 the University College made its unoccupied new buildings at Highfield available as a military hospital, for which numerous wooden huts were then erected. Photographed in front of some of them on Sunday afternoon 12 September 1915, is a group of recuperating soldiers and visitors from the South Hants Temperance Association.

Early in 1914 the Principal, Dr Hill, rented a large house and former hotel as his home and college hostel, styled Highfield Hall. On the outbreak of war he lent it for use as a Red Cross hospital. Here three nurses pose by the gates.

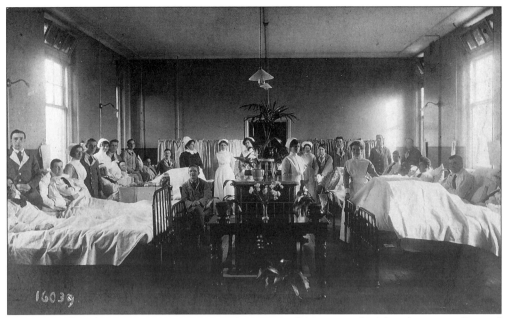

Nursing staff and army patients were smartly 'on parade' in a ward of Southampton General Hospital, posing for Shirley photographer William Pearce. The occasion may have been a 'passing out' day for men leaving after treatment.

Many sizeable houses were taken over for use as Red Cross hospitals and convalescent centres. Nellie G. Smith attended on 8 June 1917 to produce souvenir postcards of this group in the grounds of the 'The Chine', Frederick Brown's home at 70 Northlands Road.

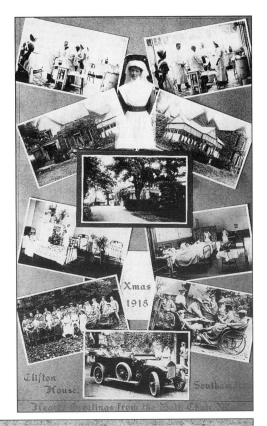

'Xmas 1918 - Hearty Greetings from the Bath Chair Man' is the message on this card, illustrating the use of Clifton House, Regents Park, as a St John's Ambulance sectional hospital. Previously accommodating St George's Catholic School for Boys from 1907-13, the house was demolished in 1930 for building the new Thorner's almshouses. The identity of the 'Bath Chair Man' remains unknown but he was presumably a local helper who gave 'walks' to servicemen recuperating from leg injuries. He also produced these verses in tribute to staff and patients.

C - stands for Clifton, that grand home of rest.
L - SISTER LILLIAN : "one of the best."
I - for the Inmates, all going strong ;
F - the brief Furlough for which they all long.
T - good old 'Tommo,' what a 'tale' he can tell us.
O - for the Outings : Carlton, Hippo, and Palace.
N - for Night Sisters—it gave us a fright when we
     heard that at Clifton 'twas 'DAY' all the night.
H - stands for HEDGES : 'some' Nurse you'll agree.
O - for the Others of the great V. A. D.
U - Sister 'U'LAND, who makes the boys querk.
S - the whole Staff, with their hearts in the work.
E - stands for Everyone who help where they can,
          Including your old friend
                    THE BATH-CHAIR MAN.

A postcard distributed by the Red Cross for their use shows captured German sailors occupying themselves at the skating rink in Shirley Road (page 98), taken over as a prisoner of war transit camp. Bevios Mount House (page 18) was similarly used to accommodate German officer prisoners.

Flag sellers on Wednesday 31 May 1916, designated 'Our Blind Heroes Flag Day' under Royal patronage. Their collections for St Dunstan's were supplemented by a charity matinee at the Palace Theatre.

As men volunteered or were conscripted for the armed services, women increasingly took their places in munitions and other essential work supporting the war effort. Only a fraction of those employed in the Pirelli cable works are shown in this section of a long panoramic photograph, *c.* 1917.

An overall view of women at the benches in a huge Pirelli workshop, *c.* 1917.

Girls on war work with Parsons Motor Co. which was based at Town Quay and associated with Parsons & Kemball Ltd who also had premises at Portwood and Woolston. The group posed for this souvenir postcard produced by Applin's Studio in Commercial Road.

Women undertook heavy and dirty work, such as wielding shovels and pushing barrows of coal and coke dust at Northam Gas Works.

Happily styled 'The Nine Ants', the 'Costume Concert Party' of the 1/9th Battalion, Hampshire Regiment comprised men named, left to right: Fry, Beeching, Suddary, White, Raynor, Mitchell (piano), Jeffers, Butler and Fry. Their T.A. unit, moblised on the outbreak of war, served on coastal defence before being sent to India in February 1916. Its concert party evidently gained wider repute, for it was photographed in the summer of 1918 on a tour of Mesopotamia, entertaining Hampshire and other troops serving there.

If the players afterwards rejoined their units in India, they would soon have faced very different duties and temperatures, for in October 1918 the 1/9th were ordered to embark from Bombay to Vladivistock, thence by rail across Siberia to Omsk, in support of the anti-Bolshevik forces of General Koltchak. Eventually withdrawn from this abortive expedition, the battalion left by ship to Vancouver, then overland across Canada and finally by transatlantic liner to reach Southampton on 5 December 1919. Having covered some 52,000 miles in nearly four years overseas, it was disbanded the same day.

In 1914-19 men of the two regular and thirty-four other battalions of the Royal Hampshire Regiment served in almost every theatre of war. Hampshire claimed a higher proportion of serving men than any other county.

Itchen Peace Day Celebrations, 30 July 1919. The First World War ended on 11 November 1918 but peace celebrations awaited German acceptance of the Treaty of Versailles on 28 June 1919. Local programmes of commemoration extended through July.

Public subscription raised £10,000 for Southampton's memorial to its 2,000 war dead. Designed by Sir Edwin Lutyens, it was unveiled on Saturday 6 November 1920. The mayor, Sidney Kimber, laid the first wreath on behalf of the organising commitee. Most other flowers were informal family tributes. This photograph was issued as a postcard by Short & Millard of Commercial Road.

Nine
From Peace to War

The years between the two world wars were generally good ones for Southampton. Port and town enjoyed the peak years of the great ocean liners, signalised in 1932-34 by the opening of the new Western Docks and the George V Graving Dock; developments at Supermarine were also highly significant. Enlarged by the incorporation in 1920 of Woolston, Sholing and Bitterne, Southampton further expanded with thousands of suburban houses, both council and private. Corporate identity was enhanced in the late 1930s by an impressive Civic Centre complex, while other aspects of progress ranged from luxury cinemas to new senior and secondary schools.

Royal visits were occasions for enthusiastic civic welcomes and expressions of popular loyalty. 'Long Live Our Prince' was the banner across the High Street between the Dolphin Hotel and Holy Rood church on 27 June 1924, when the Prince of Wales was driven through the town in the mayoral car.

SOUVENIR OF THE VISIT OF H.R.H. PRINCE OF WALES TO SOUTHAMPTON JUNE 27TH 1924.

The future Edward VIII came to inaugurate 'the World's largest floating dry dock' (page 44); this he did aboard the paddle steamer *Duchess of Fife*, snapping a ribbon to enter it. The Prince also toured the docks, Supermarine works and Imperial Airways base at Woolston.

TOC H. MARK V. BASSETT, SOUTHAMPTON.

As Toc H patron, he unveiled a tablet and lit a symbolic lamp in the house at Bassett (The Firs) given by W.S. Jones to the movement for Christian community service deriving from Talbot House, the rest centre on the Western Front, named in memory of the youngest son of the Bishop of Winchester. Demolished in 1978, Toc H Mark V is recalled by modern Talbot Close and The Firs.

H.M. The Queen at Southampton. Aug. 7th.

Queen Mary, here being received at the Royal Pier, where she had landed from Lord Inchcape's yacht, came from Cowes on 7 August 1924 to pay a private visit to Lord and Lady Swaythling at Townhill Park House.

The inauguration by the Duke and Duchess of York of the new road in front of the Civic Centre on their way to the Royal Show, 6 July 1932. They returned on 8 November for the opening of the first block of the Civic Centre, for which they had laid the foundation stone on 1 July 1930. The clock tower was completed in 1933, along with the Law Courts; the Guildhall followed in 1937 and the Art Gallery and Library in 1939.

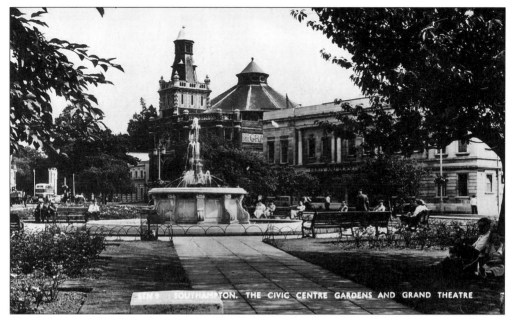

The fountain and rose garden in front of the Civic Centre were created in 1934, providing an island of tranquillity, with the Hants & Dorset bus station and the Grand Theatre in the background. All have given way to redevelopment and road works, although the fountain has been austerely re-erected outside the Art Gallery.

Transforming the Above Bar scene after demolition of the old Thorner's Charity, the complex of cinema, post office and shops, designed to complement the new Civic Centre, was speedily built in 1935 by Brazier & Son. The Forum (later ABC, then Cannon) closed in 1991; the building is now a 'super pub'.

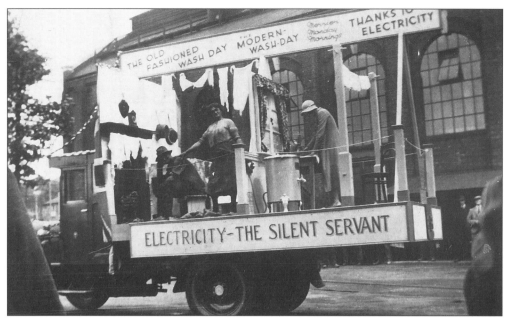

Contrasting tableaux of old-fashioned and modern washdays on a 1933 Carnival float promoting the wider used of electrical apparatus for domestic purposes, then still something of a novelty. This publicity emanated from the Corporation, which itself provided the town's electricity supply from 1896 until nationalisation in 1948.

Southampton Hospitals Carnival Week comprised an extensive programme of fund-raising events. A notable one in 1933 was the PT display by 4,000 schoolchildren, which included forming Borough Arms, Union Jack and Red Cross coloured patterns. This photograph was taken at the rehearsal; on the night, 20 June, the weather was unkind but 20,000 admiring spectators still crowded into Charlie Knott's stadium.

Invigorating paddle steamer cruises along the coast and to the Isle of Wight, also day trips to the Channel Islands and France, were very popular departures from the Royal Pier before and between the wars. A long-time favourite with excursionists was the *Lorna Doone*, 427 tons, capable of 17 knots, with a full-length promenade deck. She was taken for naval duties in both wars: returning worn out in 1946, she was laid up and scrapped.

A smart body of men were the crew of the *Lorna Doone* in the 1920s. Her elegant accommodation included a bar styled 'Half Way Doone' and a lounge called 'The Retreat'.

A new paddler added to the Red Funnel fleet in 1936 was named for Gracie Fields, who herself launched her from Thornycroft's Woolston yard on 8 April that year. The *Gracie Fields* was short-lived; requisitioned in 1939 as a Dover minesweeper, she was bombed and sunk during her Dunkirk rescue duty in May 1940.

These lucky people were enjoying a sunny cruise aboard the *Mauretania* on 24 August 1936 – for only a few shillings! She was not, of course, the luxury liner but the Red Funnel steamer formerly *Queen*, renamed by arrangement with Cunard White Star to preserve the famous name between the withdrawal of its first bearer in 1935 and the launch of the second in 1938.

THE CHILDREN'S PADDLING POOL, THE COMMON, SOUTHAMPTON. G.7980.

Nostalgic childhood delights at the paddling pool on the Common, constructed in 1937 by filling in an old reservoir (Cowherds Lake) with material excavated from the West Marlands for Civic Centre foundations. Sixty years later the pool has been reconstructed in a much more sophisticated form.

COWHERDS LAKE, Southampton
CAST STONE FOUNTAIN
Manufactured by
THE BLOKCRETE COMPANY LTD.

The centrepeice of the original pool was this delightful composition by C.H. Meadows (1868-1942), a talented sculptor, carver and moulder responsible for many memorials and other decorative works in and around Southampton. The cherub disappeared in the 1940s: the carved pedestal was removed during recent reconstruction works. They were made by the Blokcrete Company, specialists in artificial stone and cement work, established in 1920 by Walter Brazier and other local builders.

126

This aerial view of the High Street and Above Bar, *c.* 1925, highlights the long main thoroughfare centred on the Bargate, under which all traffic had to pass until new roads around it were created in the 1930s. A vanished landmark prominent on the eastern side of the High Street is the large church with tower and cupola, All Saints (page 79).

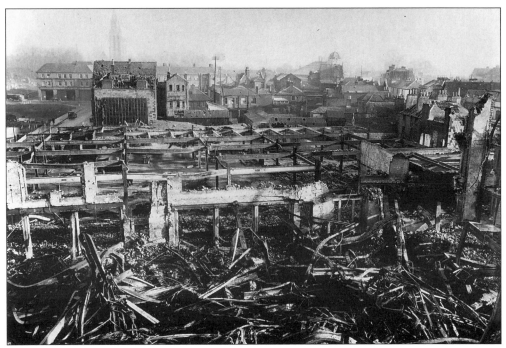

Much of central Southampton was destroyed by German bombing in 1940-41. This view, looking towards St Mary's church and the Central Hall, presents a scene of almost complete devastation.

Above Bar on 1 December 1940, after the heaviest night raid. The Prudential Assurance building was substantial enough to survive it all, happily enduring post-war redevelopment to provide a distinctive architectural heritage from the nineteenth into the twenty-first century.